NATIVE ARTISTS of NORTH AMERICA

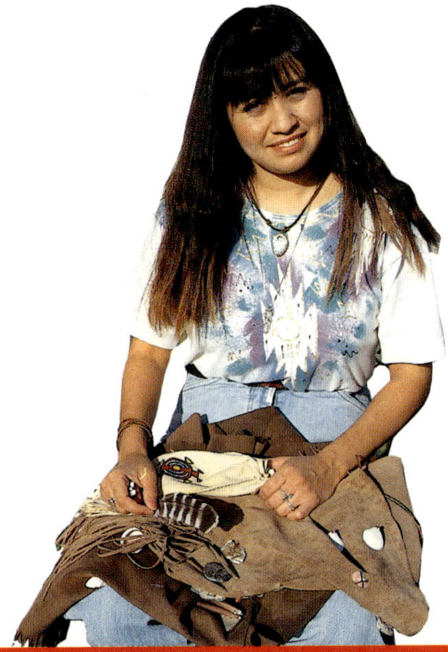

Reavis Moore

John Muir Publications
Santa Fe, New Mexico

This book is dedicated to Eliza

Many thanks to Jeffrey Bronfman, Seth Roffman and Southwest Learning Centers, Andrew Ungerleider, Rick Hill, Candy Routt, the IAIA Museum, Jodie Winsor, R. J. Joseph, Susana Valadez (anthropological consultant on the Huichols), Tony Romero, Linda Billy, Sharon Halfpound of the Cayuga Nation Office, Bertha Seyler of the Spokane Tribal Office, Robert May of the *Wellpinit* (Washington) *Independent*, John Reis, Tom Law, Rachel Howland, Nancy Gilkyson, Kay Moore, Eliza Gilkyson, and the rest of the Moore and Gilkyson families—past, present, and future.

Special thanks to the artists, Mariano, Robert, Tammy, Charlene, and Jacy and their families for sharing their lives with me.

John Muir Publications, P.O. Box 613, Santa Fe, New Mexico 87504

Text © 1993 by Reavis Daniel Moore
Illustrations and cover © 1993 by John Muir Publications
All rights reserved. Published 1993
Printed in the United States of America

First edition. First printing May 1993.

Library of Congress Cataloging-in-Publication Data

Moore, Reavis, 1951-
    Native artists of North America / Reavis Moore. — 1st ed.
      p. cm. — (Rainbow warrior artists)
    Includes index.
    Summary: Brief biographies of five talented Native Americans, discussing their background and culture and their contributions to the world of art, music, and dance.
    ISBN 1-56261-105-4 : $14.95
    1. Indians of North America—Biography—Juvenile literature. 2. Indian artists—Biography—Juvenile literature. 3. Indians of North America—Art—Juvenile literature. [1. Indians of North America—Biography.] I. Title. II. Series.
E89.M83 1993
700'.92'.273—dc20

[B]   93-16254
                                                                                  CIP
                                                                                    AC

Typeface: Benguiat, Kabel
Illustrations: Chris Brigman
Design/Typography: Ken Wilson
Printer: Guynes Printing, Albuquerque, New Mexico
Printed on recycled paper

Distributed to the book trade by
W. W. Norton & Company, Inc.
500 Fifth Avenue
New York, New York 10110

Distributed to the education market by
The Wright Group
19201 120th Avenue N.E.
Bothell, Washington 98011

Cover: Mariano Valadez of
the Huichol tribe
Photo by Seth Roffman

CONTENTS

Foreword, by LeVar Burton   4

Introduction   5

Chapter 1   **Mariano Valadez of the Huichol Tribe**   6
From the south (Mexico)—a yarn painter.

Chapter 2   **Charlene Teters of the Spokane Tribe**   14
From the north (Washington)—a visual artist.

Chapter 3   **Tammy Rahr of the Cayuga Nation**   22
From the east (New York)—a beader and doll maker.

Chapter 4   **Robert Mirabal of Taos Pueblo**   30
From the center (New Mexico)—a flute player and flute maker.

Chapter 5   **Jacy Romero of the Chumash Tribe**   38
From the west (California)—a dancer.

Glossarized Index   46

FOREWORD BY LEVAR BURTON

What is creativity? I'm sure it means something different to almost everyone, so I'll give you my definition. Creativity is that brilliant spark of life inside of me that I express in the world. How I express that creative spark is what defines me as an artist, whether it's acting or writing or telling someone how I feel in a conversation. These are all true forms of creative expression.

You might feel creative when you're painting, singing, playing basketball, or cooking. My point is this: there is no one way to be creative. Creativity has as many faces as there are human beings on the planet. It is the job of the artist to discover what form of expression suits her or him best and then create from a place of joy. That is the key. We know we are on the creative path when what we do brings us joy.

Have you ever noticed how your own moods tend to affect those around you? How your good mood can help cheer up your best friend when he or she is feeling sad? The same is true when we express ourselves creatively. As artists, when we create from that pure place of joy, we have the ability to inspire those around us to discover their own creative spark. This is the miracle of creativity. This is how we change the world.

In the Rainbow Warrior Artists series you will meet remarkable individuals from around the world. You will hear them talk about creativity and how they express it in their lives. It is my hope that their stories will help fan your creative spark into a brilliant flame that helps to light the way for all of us.

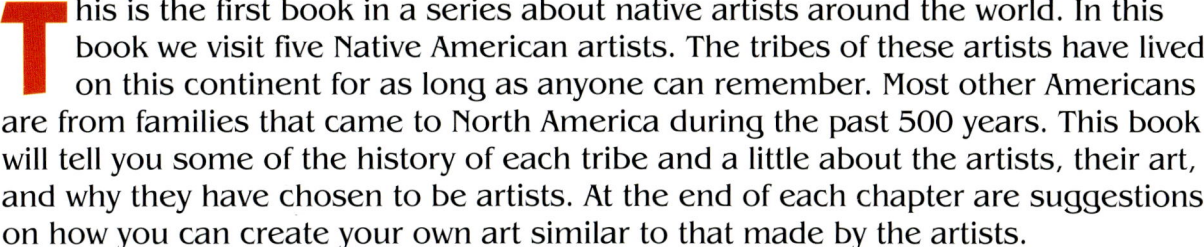
INTRODUCTION

This is the first book in a series about native artists around the world. In this book we visit five Native American artists. The tribes of these artists have lived on this continent for as long as anyone can remember. Most other Americans are from families that came to North America during the past 500 years. This book will tell you some of the history of each tribe and a little about the artists, their art, and why they have chosen to be artists. At the end of each chapter are suggestions on how you can create your own art similar to that made by the artists.

Traditional native people are artists by nature and necessity; there is little separation between art and everyday life. They create for themselves many of the things that, today, we buy at stores, such as pots, clothing, toys, and jewelry. In traditional native cultures, the people are very aware that they depend upon nature to provide food and the materials needed to create their clothing and shelters. Because of this awareness, their art usually reflects an appreciation and respect for nature and is often made for use in native religious ceremonies.

Not all native people of North America continue to live in a traditional way. Many things have changed since people from other lands began coming here. As they arrived over the last 500 years, mostly from Europe, they brought new ways of life. Unfortunately for all of us, the Europeans used their armies to force the native people to accept European culture and to abandon traditional native customs.

You will see that most Native Americans now live lives similar to yours, but the old ways have not been forgotten. The five artists profiled here, and the tribes they represent, are working to sustain the traditional ways.

WHAT TRIBE ARE YOU FROM?

We are all descendants of tribal cultures. In the past, your ancestors lived in tribes in Europe, Africa, Asia, or elsewhere. Most of the Native American values expressed in this book, like respect for nature and the Earth, were sacred to your ancestors as well. This book may inspire you to explore your own traditions, and discover your own tribal heritage.

For instance, if your ancestors were European, you may be a descendant of the Celtic (KEL•tik) tribe. Like the Native Americans, the Celts were almost destroyed by foreign armies and religions. But Celtic storytelling, music, dancing, and seasonal celebrations continue to this day in parts of Ireland, Scotland, England, and continental Europe. Even a form of the ancient language is still spoken.

As we enter the twenty-first century, we face questions about the survival of the human species. Remembering our native past and the values important to our ancestors may better prepare us for the challenges of the future.

ARE YOU AN ARTIST?

You can be an artist if you choose to be one. Listen to the artists you meet here. Look at their lives. Think about their ideas. Perhaps they will inspire you to follow your own creative path and become an artist yourself.

MARIANO VALADEZ
of the Huichol Tribe

THE HUICHOL LAND AND PEOPLE

If you travel south into Mexico from Arizona you will find the Sierra Madre Occidental Mountains. The Huichols (WEE•chols) have lived here for thousands of years. Other tribes, fleeing from Spanish invaders hundreds of years ago, came to these mountains and eventually became part of the Huichol tribe.

The Huichol homeland is mountainous. It has high deserts with pine forests, river valleys, and steep canyons. There are many different trees including oak, wild plum, and avocado. Summers are hot and winters are cold, but it never snows. The winds are strong, and the air is dry.

There is one large river, the Rio Chapalagana, and many smaller streams and natural springs. Water represents the Huichol's connection to the ocean, which is where they believe they came from. The ocean is a five day walk through the mountains, and many Huichols make this journey.

One of the amazing things about these people is that they walk almost everywhere they go. After the roads from the cities end, you must walk several hours before you come to their houses.

> *We don't know how old we are. My grandmother says we are descendants of the Aztecs. Our creation myths go back to primordial times. We know how the world began.*
>
> —Mariano Valadez

A canyon in the Huichol lands

Most Huichols do not live in towns. Large extended families live on ranches. Huichol houses are built from mud (adobe), rock, or grasses and branches. There is no electricity and no running water. The cooking is done over open fires.

Corn is plentiful (yellow, white, blue, red, or mixed). Because of the cliffs and steep hills, they sometimes pick the corn from overhead! They grow squash, beans, and chiles, and there are lots of fruit trees. The men hunt for food. The women collect wild things that go into the soup at night like herbs, grasshoppers, and wasp larvae.

The tribe comes together at temples and shrines that are very old. Shrines are often in caves or on cliffs. They contain small idols that represent the Huichol gods. People bring offerings like food, bead work, and feathers to these shrines.

The temples are large round buildings made out of mud and stone that have huge thatched roofs. A temple can hold about two hundred people. Around the temples are smaller houses. Each house is devoted to a different god. One is for the fire god, one for the Earth mother, one for the deer, and so on. Families take turns living in these houses—for five years at a time—and help with temple activities.

Huichol people in front of an adobe building

Over the years the Huichols have slowly been drawn into a world where money is needed to survive. Missionaries and government schools have encouraged the adoption of modern culture and lifestyle. Many Huichols now work outside the homeland to earn money to buy things. This has taken them away from their traditional lifestyle. But today many are returning to their traditions.

Creativity is a way of life for the Huichols. Their ceremonial clothing is decorated with different symbols from their religion, like animals and plants. Their offerings to the gods are works of art. To the Huichols, art is life and a way of honoring the sacred.

Huichol children

MARIANO VALADEZ

Mariano Valadez is a yarn painter who is helping to renew traditional Huichol art. He and his wife, Susana, run the Huichol Cultural Center. Here, people from the tribe learn traditional art forms like bead work, yarn painting, weaving, and sewing. Mariano and Susana have three children. All of the children are learning the arts of their tribe so that they can better understand the roots of their culture.

When Mariano was a small boy in the 1950s he knew nothing of the outside world.

When I was a kid I lived in a very isolated area. There were no cars, no outsiders came in, and we didn't have nice clothes. The children were mostly naked. We didn't have any toys; we made balls out of old rags.

Yet he didn't feel poor or deprived. The food was good and plentiful. There was much love and laughter in his family. But modern culture arrived and things changed for him.

When the schools and the missions started coming in, that changed a lot of things. The schools got the children interested in coming by giving them clothes. Then they built the airstrips, and the airplanes began to land, and the children would always be out there. They were the first ones to adopt modern ways.

With the changes came pressure for Mariano's father to seek work outside the Huichol homeland in order to earn money.

My father was a Shaman (a wise one, or priest). He took the family to the tobacco fields to find work. When I was a little older the family left every year to work in the fields, because we needed money to start living in the new way. Unfortunately, my father was killed in the fields.

After his father's death Mariano was taken in by a Mexican family and spent part of his time with them and part of his time in the mountains with his people. His grandmother was a storyteller, and she taught him about the Huichol way. Although he grew up with a foot in both worlds, he lived a very traditional life.

Mariano, Susana, and family

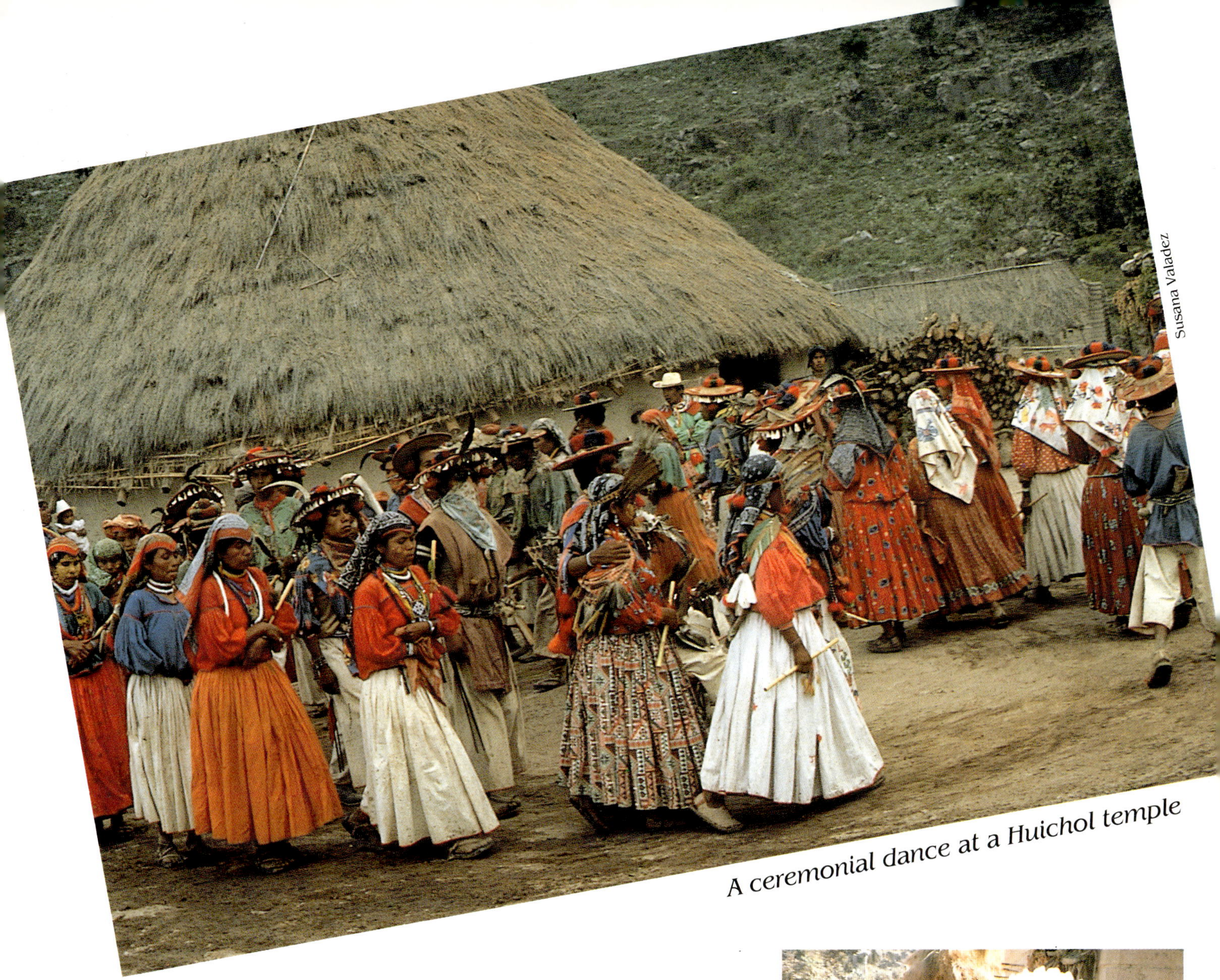

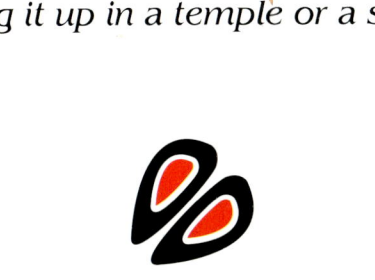

A ceremonial dance at a Huichol temple

Most of his five brothers and sisters became Shamans like their father. Mariano became a yarn painter. His artwork is part of an ancient tradition within the culture.

Ceremonial art, which is given to the gods and goddesses, was always happening. It is little things, like arrows with etchings and feather work. If you want to have many cows, you make a little yarn painting on a piece of bark or a round piece of wood, and you make a picture of lots of little cows. If you want a girlfriend you make a pretty girl. If you want a healthy corn field you make a picture of corn. Then you bring the little disk and hang it up in a temple or a shrine.

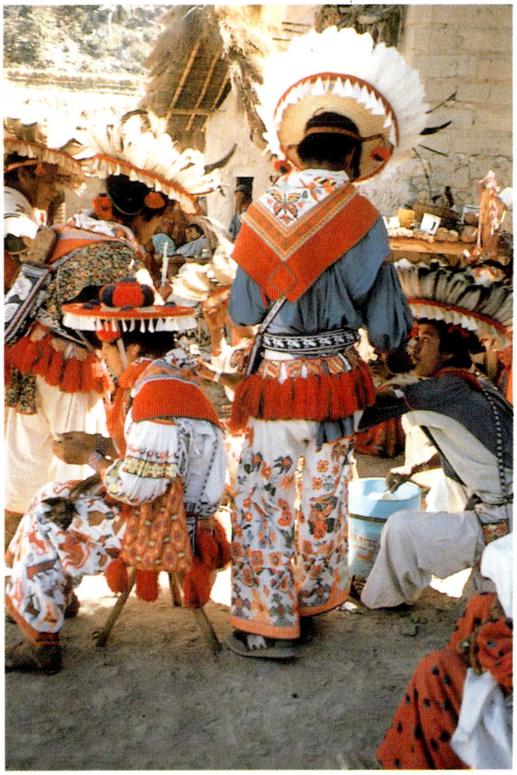

Huichol Shamans in traditional dress

MARIANO'S ART: SPEAKING VISIONS WITH PAINTINGS

Mariano has chosen the artist's path. His paintings hang in places that are far from the Huichol world. From an apartment in New York City to a museum in Santa Fe, New Mexico, his beautiful, round rainbow-colored yarn paintings carry the Huichol story.

Mariano does not use paint on canvas or use a brush in his artwork. His paintings are made of yarn. He starts by putting a sticky substance onto a round, flat wooden board. The board is usually about four feet wide. He then slowly and carefully places pieces of yarn on the sticky surface of the board. He uses many different colors of yarn. By the time he is finished, the board is filled with pictures of animals, plants, and people.

Some of Mariano's art is made to be sold and some is made to be used in Huichol ceremonies. Each painting has a special meaning. When he creates, he thinks about the meaning. In this way he makes contact with his ancestors who created in the same way. The money Mariano earns from selling his paintings goes to support the Huichol Cultural Center and to support the ceremonial activities of the tribe.

Mariano's paintings are drawn from the visions that the Shamans have during their religious ceremonies.

Everything I paint is from the visions of the wise ones. That's where I get my ideas. My art comes from the Shaman's chants. I picture what the Shamans are saying and make paintings from what I picture. The Shamans aren't singing songs that have already been written. They don't know what they are going to say until they say it. That's how I am with my art. The colors, the forms, and the designs come to me as I create. It isn't planned. It is a blissful experience for me.

Mariano's paintings depict the animals, plants, and people who make up the Huichol way of life

At the Huichol Cultural Center they teach this type of art and encourage the people to preserve their cultural ways through the arts.

Although every child learned the beading techniques, and every woman knew the weaving techniques, and every person knew yarn painting techniques, previously we couldn't afford to buy the materials and the colors.

Because of Mariano and Susana's work, the center is now filled with beautiful art. Through his artwork, Mariano brings much joy to his tribe. In his paintings he is able to bring to life things that other people only imagine. Because of the beauty of his art, he has inspired others to become yarn painters. He has taught many Huichols who are now artists themselves. The success of his art has helped the Huichol people survive. It has also helped them carry on tribal ways that might have been forgotten.

HONORING YOURSELF THROUGH ART

Mariano is a man who is comfortable living in both the traditional way and the modern way. But no matter where he travels in the modern world he always carries the Huichol traditions with him.

Mariano believes it is important to remember where you come from and to honor your roots.

When I was a child I was brought up in the traditions, but as I got older there was a temptation to leave the old ways. Many of us go out into the world, forget about who we are, don't honor the old ways, and don't listen anymore. The yarn paintings have really kept me in touch with who I am.

You may know something about the traditions of your people. Maybe your ancestors came from Africa, maybe they came from Europe, maybe Asia or South America. Wherever your people came from you have traditions too. For most people the traditional ways, or old ways of living, have been replaced by modern lifestyles. Even in a tribe like Mariano's the new ways have become strong. These new ways of living are not bad, but we need the traditional ways, too. Remembering the old ways gives us a sense of belonging and feeling of security that is often lacking in modern societies.

One of the most important values of the Huichol traditional way of living is respect for all life, including your own.

My message to children is to honor who you are and to appreciate who you are. There are many ways of doing this. Art is an important one.

A Huichol woman in ceremonial dress

ACTIVITY PAGE

MAKE YOUR OWN YARN PAINTINGS

You can learn to make yarn paintings similar to those made by Mariano.

You will need the following materials.
- A piece of cardboard.
- Some paste or glue.
- Some pieces of brightly colored yarn.
- A pencil.

Before you begin think about what you want your picture to look like. What animals or plants or people will you put in it?

Step 1. Draw the picture you want to make on the piece of cardboard with your pencil. You don't need to be too careful, because you will cover the drawing with yarn.

Step 2. Decide what color of yarn to use for each part of the picture. Use your imagination and have fun.

Step 3. Spread a thin layer of paste or glue over a small part of your drawing on the cardboard. Make sure you can still see the drawing under the paste.

Step 4. Lay the yarn on the glue along the lines of the picture that you drew. Fill in the solid parts of the picture with more yarn. Then, spread more paste or glue onto another section, and place more yarn over your drawing.

Experiment with different techniques. How large a patch of glue works best? What thickness of glue works best? When do long pieces of yarn work best? When is thin yarn better?

Experiment. Have fun. Soon, you will become a good yarn painter, and you will have many nice gifts to give to friends and family.

Remember, the Huichols make many of their yarn painting as offerings to the gods.

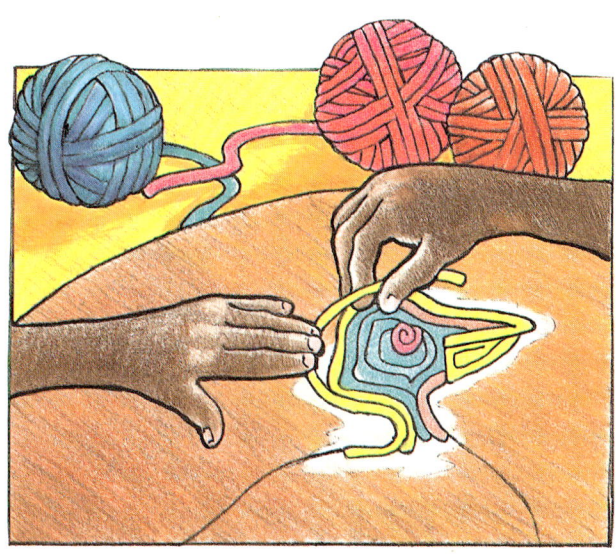

13

CHARLENE TETERS
of the Spokane Tribe

THE SPOKANE LAND AND PEOPLE

The Spokane (spoh•CAN) tribe lives in the state of Washington in the northwest United States. A tribal legend says they have lived there since the beginning of human memory. The native people of that area also include the Colville, Coeur D'Alene, and Kalispell tribes.

Together these tribes were known as the Salmon People because of the fish in the Columbia and other rivers of the area. They say there were once so many salmon that when they spawned, the rivers were red, and you could walk across on the backs of the fish.

They are also plateau people, because they live on a high plain at the foot of the great jagged Cascade Mountains. The land is dry and covered with sagebrush and giant Ponderosa pine trees. Many of the plants and herbs that grew here are now extinct. In the old days the tribe collected these plants for food and medicine. They also fished and hunted for food.

Traditionally, the Spokane people migrated with the seasons along the eastern

The land of the Spokane tribe

I believe that art is the highest form of communication. Artists have always been the conscience of their nations.

—Charlene Teters

Cascades from Canada down into Oregon, Idaho, and Montana. The people lived in huts of willow wood and reeds—shaped like domes. Later, they adopted the teepees of the plains people.

In their sacred dances many animals are represented: the eagle, hawk, bluejay, mockingbird, and owl from the sky; the coyote, badger, and mole from the ground; and the salmon from the water. Dance has always been at the heart of the tribe's religion. Through dance, mythology and history are expressed. The sacred arts—dancing, singing, and drumming—are all part of a language that speaks beautifully of the Earth and the passing seasons of human life.

Traditionally, education in the tribe is done by the storytellers. They are the historians and keepers of the sacred truths. Some stories, like coyote stories, are only told during winter when nature becomes quiet and families gather together.

A Spokane traditional dancer

In the 1700s the Spokane people first met the Europeans. In the beginning the trappers, mainly French, settled nearby and adopted the tribe's ways. Later, gold was discovered on tribal lands, and many miners came to take it. The chiefs encouraged the people to live peacefully with the newcomers, but the tribe's young warriors tried to stop the miners from taking the gold. The U.S. government sent troops to protect the miners. The army had superior weapons and soon took control of the tribe and their land.

For years after that the tribe had no land of its own. The people became prisoners of war, because they wouldn't sign a treaty with the U.S. government. Finally, the tribe was given a reservation. Like all other tribes, they were forbidden to practice their religion, but the people continued to dance and sing in secret. By 1900 there were only 750 people left in the tribe.

Today, the tribe lives on a small reservation where they continue their traditional ways and work to educate and take care of all of their people. The current tribal population is over two thousand people.

CHARLENE TETERS

Charlene Teters was born and raised in the city of Spokane, Washington. Her mother is Spokane and her father is Dutch. As a child she spent time on the reservation with her grandmother and other relatives.

When Charlene was young she thought her grandmother was like everybody else's.

My grandmother lived in a house that had cardboard and tar paper on the inside walls. She didn't have electricity until I was about twelve. I remember because after she got it we brought a television with us so we could watch cartoons. We went to her house every week and filled buckets of water, because she didn't have plumbing. By the time I was in the fifth grade I remember feeling ashamed of her. There was pressure to be like everyone else and think of her way of life as backward, something to be thrown away. Now, that makes me very angry and sad.

As Charlene grew older she came to understand the beauty and power of her tribal traditions and culture and to respect the wisdom of her grandmother, who was an honored storyteller in the tribe.

As a teenager, she married a man from a nearby tribe and had two children. Her husband was often drunk and violent toward her and the children. With the help of her brothers, she broke free from the cycle of alcoholism and family violence that affects many people of all cultures.

Then Charlene returned to school to study art. In 1984 she joined artists from other tribes at the Institute of American Indian Arts (IAIA) in Santa Fe, New Mexico. She graduated from IAIA and completed her bachelor's degree at the College of Santa Fe.

Charlene was then invited to study at the University of Illinois.

Children at a Spokane pow wow

It was difficult to go into an environment where there were only three Native Americans in a school of 40,000 students where the sports teams are called the Fighting Illini.

The Illini were a group of Native American tribes in the Illinois area that were driven to extinction.

At a basketball game she and her children saw the team mascot, Chief Illiniwek, a white student who pretended to do native dances in a headdress with ninety eagle feathers. She was offended by the "chief" and the fans with painted faces.

What I saw in my children was a blow to their self-esteem. There was even a tavern that had a sign saying "Home of the drinking Illini" that showed a drunken Indian falling down.

Charlene informed university officials that possession of eagle feathers by non-natives is illegal under a federal law that protects endangered species. The school replaced them with chicken feathers but refused to change the name of the sports teams.

In 1991 she graduated from the university with a master's degree in fine art and went to Washington, D.C., to work with the National Congress of American Indians.

Charlene returned to the IAIA in 1992 to become Director of Student Placement and Alumni Affairs. In this role she works closely with artists from many tribes.

A Spokane elder in traditional ceremonial dress

CHARLENE'S ART: COMMUNICATION

Charlene is a painter who often combines objects with her art. Charlene does not create her art to sell to others. She creates it to communicate ideas.

I am interested in making artwork that addresses issues and causes people to think. My work is intended to bring attention to those things that are destroying our culture.

In addition to being a painter, Charlene creates artistic settings using objects like bricks, toys, and jewelry in combination with each other. These settings can be walked through and touched, allowing the viewer to become more involved with the art.

Charlene's evolution as an artist has been personal and political. She has gone from being an abused wife to becoming a national spokesperson for native people and an educator. With her voice and artwork she challenges ideas that limit the social progress and misrepresent the cultural history of her people. She believes that artists are responsible for creating understanding and presenting the truth through their work.

I believe that art is the highest form of communication. Artists have always been the conscience of their nations.

Part of being Native American is to create. Not just to create art objects, but to change things from the Earth into things we put into or onto our bodies. My grandmother was a storyteller. My grandfather and my uncle were spiritual leaders. I think of them as creative people. They were always creating with plants and

A painting from Charlene's Warrior Woman series.

18

beads, and other things. These were my role models, so it was a natural step to go into art.

When Charlene left home to attend the IAIA she was exposed to new influences. As part of a community of artists from different tribes, she received support and guidance. She discovered her real power as an artist and as a woman. Her work from that period is mainly paintings of Native American women that show their role in keeping families together and continuing native traditions. These paintings came out of her own experiences as a woman who had to struggle to survive, while protecting and raising her children.

I came from an environment where my children and I were being abused. When I first came to the Institute my work was about reclaiming my dignity as a woman. It was about women being the center of family, the strength of family, and the center of learning and preservation of culture.

The battles Charlene fought at the University of Illinois also influenced her artwork. In modern American culture native people often are shown as bloodthirsty savages and drunks. Images in cartoons and comic books, on television and in films, combined with a lack of accurate native history have kept these wrong ideas alive. The artwork Charlene created at the university showed how these false images hide the true identity of native people. She did this by putting cartoon images of native people on top of paintings of her family, so that you have to look around or through the cartoon images to see the real person.

What I was trying to say in that body of work is that Indian people are real people that are alive today in the 20th century. The false images are so powerful that people cannot see us as we really are.

From Charlene's "What We Know About Indians" series. The cartoon in front is of an Indian used at the University of Illinois. Hidden behind it is a picture of her Uncle Frank.

DOORS WILL OPEN

Family and tribal tradition have shaped Charlene's art. Her father, a painter himself, did not want her to become an artist. He was afraid she wouldn't be able to support herself financially. Yet in her tribe she saw people creating art as a way of life. She chose art, and the communication of ideas, despite the possibility she would not earn much money from it.

Her paintings and other art inspire us to discuss and debate the issues of human dignity and freedom. Her artwork is about Native Americans, but her message is for people everywhere who are victims of cruelty and greed.

Each of us has a story to communicate, and every story is of equal importance. When you create, you tell your story. You shape your world with a picture or a word or a movement. Your art can help change the world.

You may be told at school or home that art should be secondary. I found that I felt more whole when I followed my own creative urges. My elders say that if you are doing the right thing, the doors will open for you. If you feel strongly about expressing yourself in art, you should follow that road.

Charlene with her daughter, Kristal

ACTIVITY PAGE

EYE–TO–HAND DRAWING

This activity is recommended by Charlene to help you learn how to draw. If you already draw well, this will help you improve. She suggests that you practice drawing without looking at the paper! It will improve your hand-to-eye coordination and help you observe your subject better.

Step 1. You will need a pencil and a piece of paper without lines. Find something that you would like to draw. Your subject can be something in nature like a tree, a plant, a leaf, or an animal. Or, you may want to draw a friend or a family member.

Step 2. Before you start to draw, very carefully study the outline of your subject. Then put the point of your pencil near the top of the paper.

Step 3. Keep your eyes on your subject, and begin to draw the outline, or the outside edges, of it. Don't worry about the fine details at this time—just the outline. Draw your subject in one continuous line without looking at the paper until you are finished.

Step 4. Once you have completed your outline take your pencil off the paper and look at what you have drawn. Your drawing may look funny or like a cartoon. It may not even make any sense to someone else. Don't worry! No one does well at this exercise in the beginning. But if you practice this every day you will soon become much better at it.

Step 5. After you have completed the outline, reposition your pencil, look back at your subject, and try to fill in some of the details without looking at the paper.

TAMMY RAHR
of the Cayuga Nation

THE CAYUGA LAND AND PEOPLE

In and around the area that is now known as New York state, in the northeastern United States, live the six nations of the Iroquois Confederacy. Iroquois (EAR•uh•quoy) is actually a French word. The people of these nations call themselves Haudenosaunee (hoh•DON•o•SHOH•nee) or "the People of the Long House." The long houses were huge round-roofed apartment buildings that the people slept in. They were shared community spaces with several hearths. Today, the long houses are the meeting places.

The original boundaries of this great people extended to Canada in the north, Pennsylvania in the south, Ohio in the west, and the Atlantic Ocean in the east. The Cayuga (ky•OO•guh) lived in the east of this territory.

The land is rich with lakes, rivers, and forests. There are pine, oak, and maple trees. Giant turtles, great blue heron, bear, white-tailed deer, beaver, wolves, and hawks inhabit the land. But today, there is also acid rain and many endangered species of plants and animals.

Cayuga Lake

I've always been a maker. I had to have something to play with. I was always making dolls out of clothespins, or sticks, or rocks. I'd even try to have pet ants for the day. I didn't have a real attraction for the leftover toys, the headless Barbies and stuff like that, that were around the house. So I spent a lot of time in the woods.

—Tammy Rahr

A waterfall on the traditional Cayuga lands

Even though human beings have lived on this land for thousands of years, most of this destruction has come to pass in the past 500 years, since the arrival of the European people.

Iroquois leaders are renowned for their diplomacy. They established one of the first democratic governments in the world. Unlike European countries and even the United States, women have had an equal say, what we call the vote, for many centuries. When the United States was being formed, the founding fathers borrowed ideas about governing from the Iroquois and put them in the constitution. One of the greatest achievements of these people was that the six tribes lived together in peace.

An example of the goodwill of the Iroquois people is the way in which the Tuscarora nation became part of the confederacy. The Tuscarora people used to live in the southeastern United States. In the early 1700s the tribe was suffering from a lack of food and was threatened by disease. The Iroquois Confederacy invited the Tuscaroras to join them. The Iroquois gave them land and made them members of the confederacy.

The Cayuga nation has its own unique language and its own traditions. However, over the centuries the language and customs have become mixed with those of other Iroquois nations, especially their neighbors, the Seneca.

Today, there are about 450 people in the Cayuga tribe. The members of the tribe are spread out across the country. None of the tribe now lives in the Cayuga Lake area, which was their traditional homeland. In fact, the tribe has no reservation or tribal lands. The Cayuga people were moved off of their land by the U.S. government. Currently, the tribe is fighting the government for the return of a portion of their land so that they may again have a tribal home.

The Jim Sky Iroquois Dancers at the Iroquois Indian Festival in Howes Cave, New York

TAMMY RAHR

Tammy Rahr is a bead worker and maker of traditional dolls and cradleboards, which are used to carry infants.

My Indian name is Deyehsuhhaaduhheetuh (day•EH•suh•ha•duh•HEE•tuh). What that means is "she's mashing beans."

You could say that Tammy didn't become an artist, she's always been one. Growing up in the country, she spent most of her time outdoors making things from leaves, flowers, and dirt. Nature was her medium.

I don't know where my creativity came from, but it was always there. We didn't have a lot of money, so there weren't a lot of toys. If I wanted to play with something, I had to create it. I was the artist, the weirdo. I drew a lot. I won a lot of coloring contests. The prizes were always a big bag of candy.

Today, Tammy is a highly respected Iroquois traditional artist whose bead work, corn husk dolls, and cradleboards were presented in her own show at the Smithsonian Institution in New York. She has also won first place awards at the famous Santa Fe Indian Market. She is a sought-after speaker on native rights and traditional native arts as well.

Her interest in her tribe's traditions and culture developed as she grew older. When she was a child, her family lived like most American families. In her teen years they moved from the woodlands of New York state to San Bernadino, California, outside Los Angeles. There she encountered the intensity of life in urban America.

We moved to a big city, in the early '70s, with all the '60s overflow, peace protests, the civil rights movement, and people of color—people that looked like me. Things were happening that I only had a notion about back home. I started becoming a little more aware of what was going on in the world.

After a time the family returned to New York and Tammy was faced with another lesson in growing up fast.

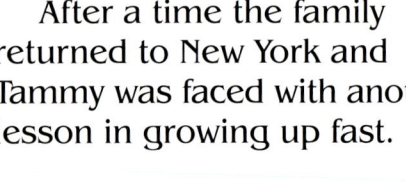

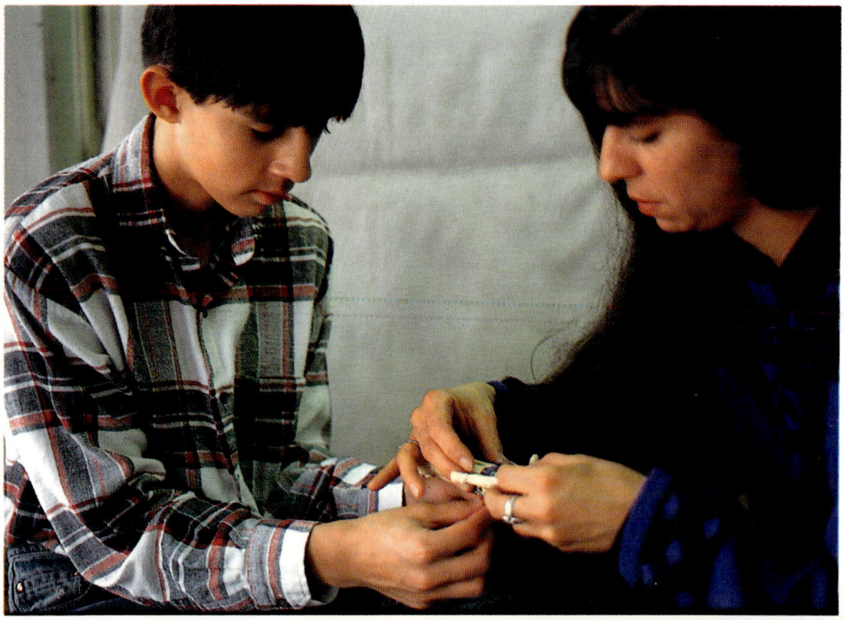

Tammy and her son, David John

I was labeled a gifted kid. They expected a lot out of me at school. As an experiment they sent me to college when I was only fourteen. It didn't work at that age, but I finished with a high school diploma and some college credit. By that time, I was so put off by the school counselors and psychologists that I quit school and went to work. I did a lot of things, from restaurant to office work.

Despite the difficulties that Tammy had in school she still believes in education.

I think you should get your formal education out of the way early. I'm not saying that the learning process ever stops, or that it's ever too late, but do as much as you can while you're young.

When she was young, Tammy had her son, David John. Eventually she and David moved to Santa Fe, New Mexico, so she could study at the Institute of American Indian Arts (IAIA). After graduation she stayed in Santa Fe where she is still active with the IAIA and its museum.

Tammy works on a traditional cornhusk doll

TAMMY'S ART: CHILDREN AND NATURE

Tammy's experiences as a child have influenced her art and her life as an adult.

One of my big concerns is children. I have a twelve-year-old son that I'm raising alone. I see kids being turned out into the street, throw away children. Throw away everything. We're a throw away society. I don't know when it became O.K. to start throwing away kids. Native American children are facing hard times. We have the highest teen suicide rate of any group of people. One out of every six Native American kids will attempt suicide, and half of them will succeed.

Her research found that Native American children have very low self-esteem. Tammy's artwork is designed to help native children overcome their lack of self-esteem by giving them a sense of who they are and where they come from.

I have been creating toys for kids. Some of these toys are Indian dolls, real Indian dolls. They're not plastic dolls made to look like dark-skinned people or people of color with phony Indian clothes.

She also combines traditional Native American and modern American toys. This helps Native American children feel that their old ways are equal to the new ways.

One of the toys that I create is the cradleboard. The cradleboards don't have little Indian dolls on them, they have modern dolls on them. The children are being given a traditional toy that you could put a GI Joe on. It gives them a sense of pride in who they are. The toys also help them to understand some of the traditional techniques.

Another area of concern for her that has become a theme in her artwork is the preservation of the natural world. As a child, Tammy learned about the plants and trees that covered the countryside around her home. As the years went by she learned to include

A cornhusk doll

A cradleboard

26

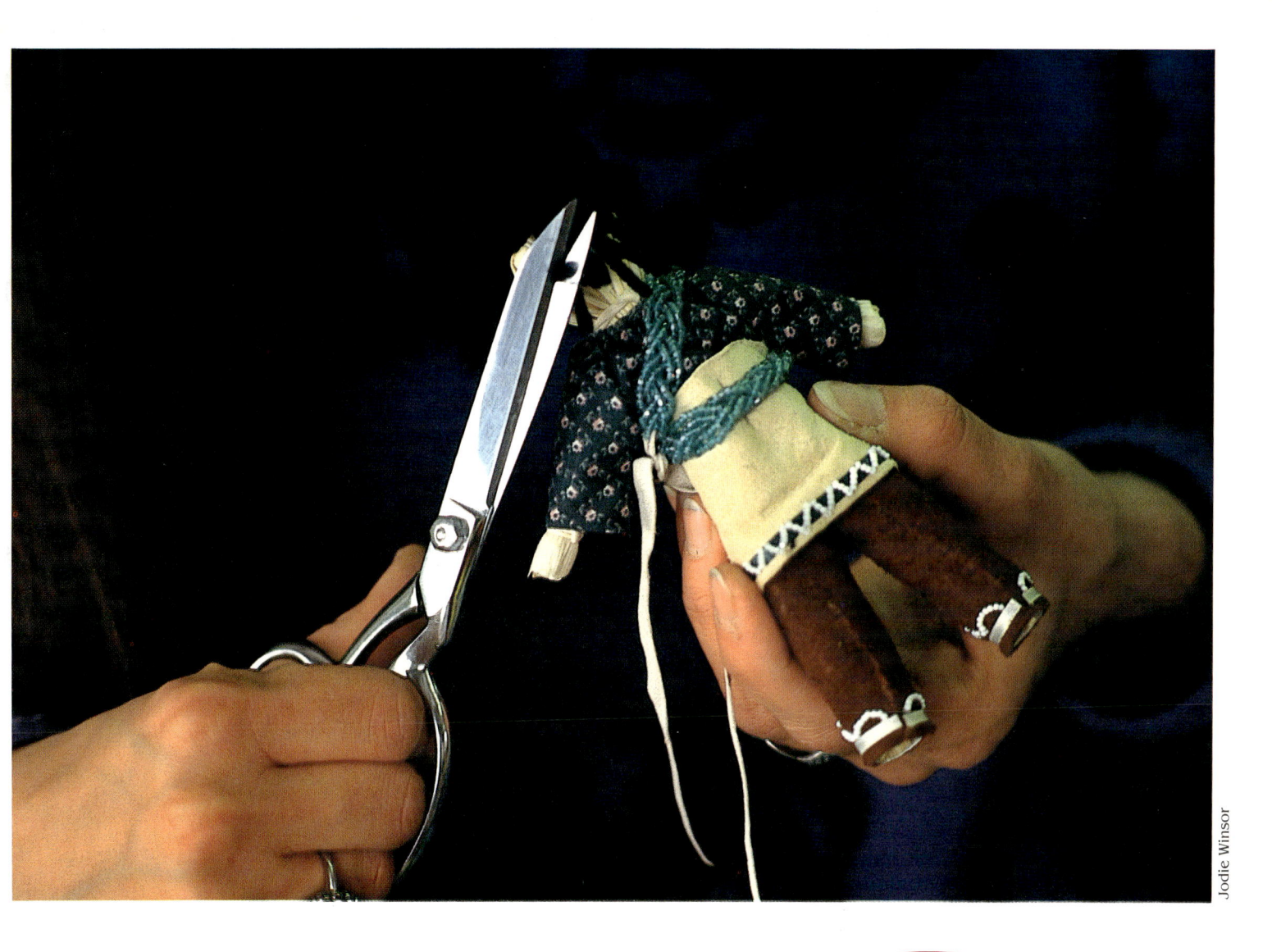

images of nature in her artwork. Today, many of these plants and trees are in danger of becoming extinct. She uses these images in her work to communicate to the younger generation that these beautiful forms of life will not be able to survive unless we care for them. On her cradleboards you see trillium flowers, wild strawberries, grapes, ferns, and even the leaves of the oak, elm, and maple trees.

The real hard fact is that this planet is being threatened by us. But we will die before she will. She will throw us off first.

An example of Tammy's bead work

YOU WILL FIND THE ANSWERS

Tammy's connection to her people's traditions and culture are themes that run through her work. But she also lives in today's world.

I don't go to the mountain and seek visions. I'm thirty-something. I live in the United States. I drive a car. I like to go to concerts. I think I have a spiritual connection with my creator and it's very personal for me. I try to share that with people. I try to help people. I try to make things that are pleasing to look at, but I also want them to have a function and a meaning. That meaning is very personal. You almost have to talk to me to understand the pieces. I have a need for art. I have a need to create. It's like therapy to me.

Inside of each of us, inside of you, is the same creative urge. Sometimes we create with our imaginations. We think and dream of people and places and things. Making art is taking dreams and thoughts and bringing them to life.

Tammy Rahr took the dreams of her childhood and turned them into artwork that touches many people. In bringing beauty to others she also brings it to herself. Her art has brought her many friendships and experiences. Along the way young people ask her for advice. This is what she tells them:

Never stop asking questions! Don't let anybody tell you to stop asking questions. You might not get the answers handed to you, but you will find your answers if you seek them out.

ACTIVITY PAGE

SEED BEADING

With a few simple materials you can create bead work similar to that created by Tammy. This page shows you how to create a necklace or bracelet out of seeds and beans.

You will need the following things:
- A spool of thread. Any color will do, but try to find thread that is strong so it won't break easily.
- A sewing needle.
- A sewing thimble that fits on your finger.
- Dried beans, and vegetable or fruit seeds like corn or watermelon. Any sort of seeds will work.
- A bowl of water.

Be sure to get as many different kinds of seeds as possible. A variety of different colored seeds and beans will make your beading more fun.

Step 1. If the seeds are hard, you will need to soak them in a bowl of water until they are soft enough to push a needle completely through them. Some seeds, like beans, may have to be soaked overnight.

Step 2. While they are soaking, take some time to think about what you want your necklace or bracelet to look like and how long it should be.

Step 3. When the seeds are soft enough, take them out of the water and make a little hole in the middle of them with the needle. Be very careful not to stick yourself with the needle. A thimble can be very useful to help you push the needle through the seeds. After making holes in the seeds large enough for the thread to go through, let them dry again.

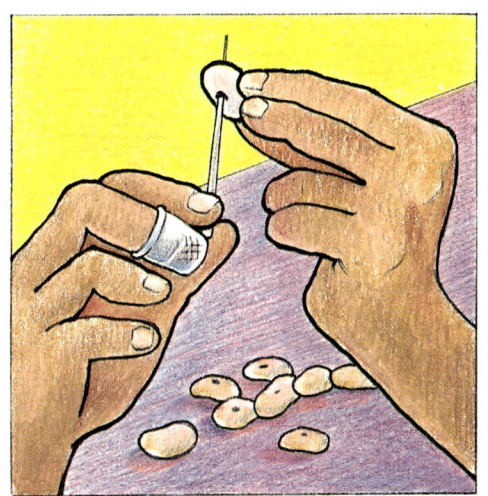

Step 4. Next, thread the needle with a piece of thread that is longer than the necklace or bracelet you want to make. Be sure to leave enough thread to tie the ends together after you have strung the beads. You can make a stronger piece by doubling the thread. When you have enough seeds on a string to make a bracelet or a necklace, take the needle off the thread, and tie the two ends of the string together.

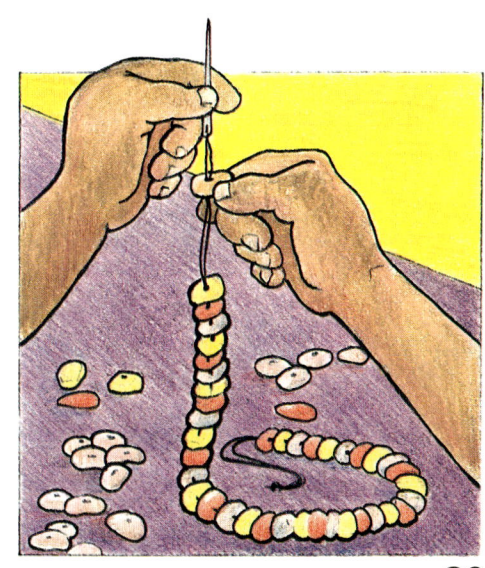

ROBERT MIRABAL
of Taos Pueblo

TAOS PUEBLO LAND AND PEOPLE

In the southwestern United States there is a place where mountains meet the high desert. Fragrant sagebrush stretches out in every direction across rolling mesas. Eagles glide freely through the Rio Grande River gorge that cuts across the desert floor. Overlooking this vast expanse is the majestic Taos Mountain. At the foot of this mountain is Taos (TA•ohs) Pueblo, one of the oldest communities in North America. The pueblo is near the town of Taos, in northern New Mexico. Through dance, song, and prayer the people of this tribe honor the land and remember their ancestors.

Through the middle of the pueblo runs a small river where people still gather as they did in distant times. In the mountains above the pueblo are hidden lakes and waterfalls surrounded by pine forests. Higher up are small pine trees that grow twisted from the wind and look like people sitting with blankets wrapped over their shoulders. These places are sacred to the Taos Pueblo people.

No one knows for sure when the pueblo came into being. Its origins are hidden in the mists of time. It may have been thousands of years ago

There are a lot of books written about Taos Pueblo, people trying to find the mysticism, the magic, the inspiration. Coming from there, it's something that you live with every single day. I like to see it from a child's point of view that it's just a place where people live. A place where they do ceremony. A place where they laugh. A place where they die.

—Robert Mirabal

Taos Mountain rises behind Taos Pueblo

that the first people made their home in this valley.

The people built their homes from mud, called adobe today. Some of the buildings are three stories tall. These ancient dwellings have been cared for and preserved over the tribe's history and today stand as reminders of the power of community. But these buildings are not monuments to an earlier time. They are homes occupied by many of the tribe members. They live as their ancestors lived, without electricity or plumbing, within rooms made of earth.

An adobe home in Taos Pueblo

Until this century, the Taos people depended on agriculture and the animals and plants of the area for survival. At one time huge herds of buffalo moved across the mesas here. The people still honor them by performing the buffalo dance and by caring for a small herd of this now-endangered animal. Deer, elk, black bear, wild turkeys, grouse, and native trout are a few of the animals that have helped sustain the tribe.

In the fields outside the village grows a cornucopia of foods. There is white and blue corn, squash, pumpkins, and beans. Plums, blueberries, and raspberries grow wild in the mountains. There are orchards of apples, peaches, and other fruits that were introduced in recent centuries. In earlier times the whole family would work in the fields. But since the children are now required to go to school, the fields have grown smaller, because the whole family has not been available to farm them.

Life at Taos Pueblo has at times been very difficult. As is true of all Native American tribes, over the centuries the people have faced invading armies and foreign religions. Many times they have had to defend their homes and families. Their continued kindness and hospitality to outsiders shows their respect for all life.

Children join in a traditional dance at the Taos Pueblo Pow Wow

ROBERT MIRABAL

Robert Mirabal is a flute player and flute maker. His flutes are traditional Native American wood instruments. Although Robert learned his art in the shelter of Taos Pueblo, his music has taken him across America and around the world. Wherever he travels and performs he carries the stories and songs of his home. He also carries with him a deep love and respect for the land. Robert was born in 1966.

We were probably the last generation to see the way the Pueblo was a long time ago. There was no electricity, no running water. We didn't have a car. There was no TV. We learned the traditional way of life. Food could be scarce, and we learned to honor it in a very special way. I grew up with a lot of relatives all around me. It seemed like everybody was happy, everybody was sharing, because nobody had more than anyone else.

Creativity takes many forms for a young man raised at Taos Pueblo. Each child is taught to sing and dance, and the ceremonial life of the pueblo gives him or her an opportunity to practice these arts with the entire community. In addition, a child learns about the artistic expression of ceremonial dress. As a teenager Robert's creative passion was acting.

I wanted to be an actor, so I did a lot of acting in high school. I did a play about becoming the first Indian president. It was a comedy. I wrote a lot of it. There was a lot of radical energy inside me. Eventually, I felt really weird about how Indians were portrayed in movies, and I said: Aw, forget this, man. I ain't gonna be an Indian actor dressed up in skins and feathers."

While growing up Robert saw the pueblo change. Government housing programs spread out from the inner cities to rural tribes. Inexpensive modern homes were built, and with them came electricity,

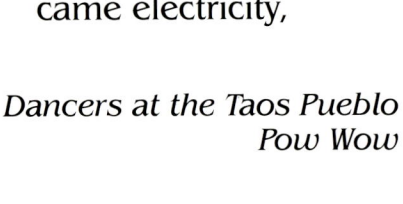

Dancers at the Taos Pueblo Pow Wow

telephones, bills, rent, and a greater need for money. Within a few years the new dwellings started to fall apart. It is odd that the original pueblo buildings are hundreds of years old and in better condition than United States government housing that is less than ten years old.

Robert also witnessed a change in the types of foods his people ate. The tribe had an almost totally natural diet until the government began giving them surplus foods.

We were raised on the government food. It's real sugary and real salty. It tastes awful. I think it may be feeding the heart and diabetic problems we're prone to. In the past, about the only sugar we had was blueberries, chokecherries, and, in the summer, honey."

Like many native people today Robert grew up in two worlds, the outside world and the traditional world of the pueblo. Today his music and life represent a bridge between these two realities.

This horno oven, made of adobe, is used to bake bread

Taos Pueblo sits at the foot of Taos Mountain

33

ROBERT'S ART: BREATHING THROUGH THE FLUTE

When Robert Mirabal walks on stage there is an electricity that runs through the room. He reaches out and draws his audience into his music and stories. It may be an audience of thousands of people in a theater or a handful of young people at a school. No matter the numbers, he works his magic, drawing people into a greater awareness of life and their own creative powers.

I had always been into music. We had a teacher in grade school who played forty different instruments. So, I went from a guitar to a saxophone, to a clarinet, to a piano, learning the basics. I bought my first Indian flute at an auction when I was 18. I didn't have any girlfriends, but I had this flute. I learned how to play it, and I learned how to make it. I consider it God's gift, so I always honor it that way. God came down and said: "O.K., no more abuse, no more fighting and tearing up your life. Here's a flute for you. Something you can build that will sustain you in your existence with your culture and the expression of the new world."

Music breaks down barriers. It has taken him to many places and into many cultures.

I really owe my life to those flutes. It's interesting how they just opened doors everywhere. It became something so much stronger than I ever thought.

Art is a way of life for Robert. His creative expression is directly connected to his beliefs and lifestyle. He sees art as basic to our human existence. Artists are historians, storytellers, and communicators. They remind us of what happened in our past, wake us up to what is happening now, and inspire us to dream and work toward our future.

Robert's art is tied to the Earth and to his culture.

Robert works on a handmade flute

Great care is required to make a flute that both sounds and looks beautiful

The most fascinating painting you'll ever see is not of a building, or a city, or a human being. It is of nature. Nature has been created by a higher creator. We can only see it, try to paint it or play music about it, and be historians of it.

Unlike many musicians, fame and fortune are not what Robert seeks.

I don't need to be rich from my music. I am rich with my culture and our land. The culture led us to create the art, the religion, and the traditions.

YOU HAVE SOMETHING THAT NOBODY ELSE HAS

Knowledge of our ancestors and the Earth is available to each of us, no matter where we live. You may have to search to come to an understanding of your ancestors. If you live in a city you may even have to search to find the Earth. But you will find it if you look.

Creativity can help you find what you seek. For Robert Mirabal, culture, land, and creating have always been part of his life. You may find clues for your own life in his words:

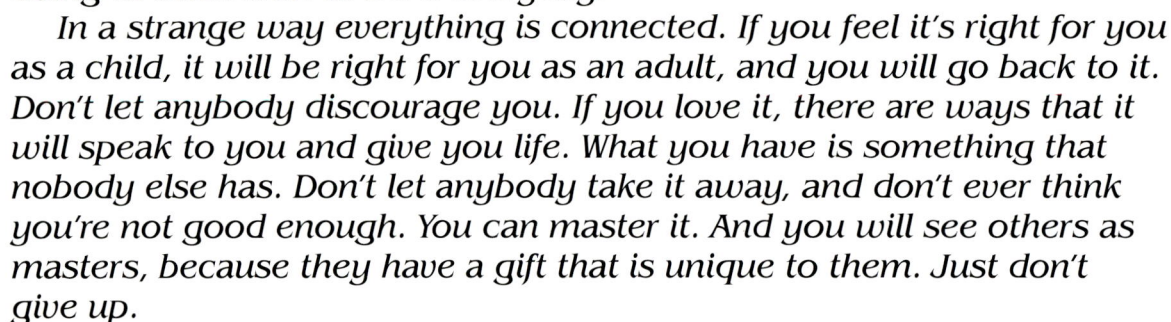

If you find something you like, and you're not good at it, just keep doing it. Stick with it. Do it everyday.

In a strange way everything is connected. If you feel it's right for you as a child, it will be right for you as an adult, and you will go back to it. Don't let anybody discourage you. If you love it, there are ways that it will speak to you and give you life. What you have is something that nobody else has. Don't let anybody take it away, and don't ever think you're not good enough. You can master it. And you will see others as masters, because they have a gift that is unique to them. Just don't give up.

Robert with drummer Reynaldo Lujan

ACTIVITY PAGE

TRACKING EARTH'S SONG

The way that Robert composes his music is by listening to the sounds of nature and then recreating them on his flute together with other musicians and instruments. He calls this tracking nature's song.

Step 1. Find a peaceful place in nature in the woods, by a river, on a hill, or in a park. Find a place that is away from the noise of the city. Sit quietly and listen for the song of the Earth. You may hear a low droning sound or a high-pitched sound. You may hear the wind whistling through the trees or the grasses. Put your ear to a tree and listen carefully. Listen for the sound of bees, insects, and birds. If you are in a wild place listen for the cry of wild animals.

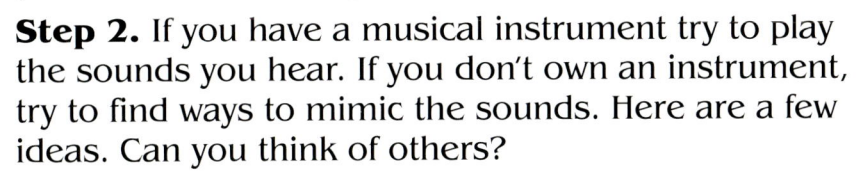

Step 2. If you have a musical instrument try to play the sounds you hear. If you don't own an instrument, try to find ways to mimic the sounds. Here are a few ideas. Can you think of others?

- To mimic the sound of the wind in the trees, cut a piece of paper so that it looks like fringe on a leather jacket. Now, gently blow across the fringed paper to make a sound like leaves in the wind.

- To mimic the sound of a gently flowing creek, slowly pour water from one container into another one. Experiment with different types and sizes of containers to learn the different sounds they make.

- Make whistling sounds that mimic the sounds of the birds.

How can you mimic the chirp of a cricket? How can you mimic the howl of the wolf?

Step 3. It is especially fun to gather several of your friends together and each make a different sound from nature. Can you combine these sounds to create your own nature song?

Now you are a tracker of Mother Nature's song.

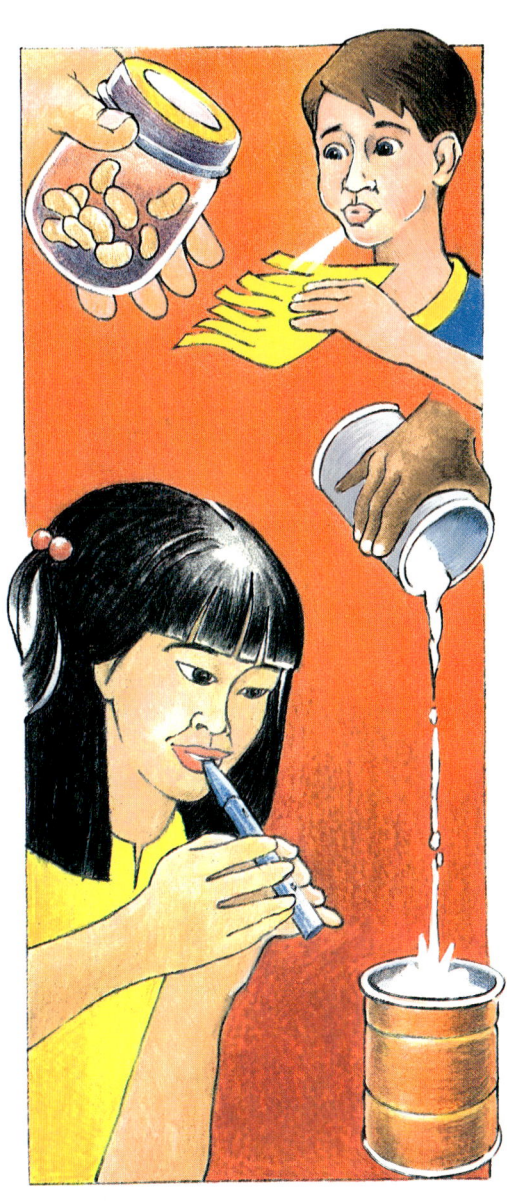

37

JACY ROMERO of the Chumash Tribe

THE CHUMASH LAND AND PEOPLE

The great Chumash (CHOO•mash) tribe once lived all along the coast of California as well as on nearby islands. Their tule (TOO•lee) grass and willow huts filled villages from the north to the south.

Their tomals (toh•MALS), or fishing canoes, plied the waters in harmony with the dolphin, swordfish, and marlin—all sacred creatures that were never hunted. When the body of a dead whale washed ashore, all of its parts were used with respect, including the bones, which became musical instruments.

The people wore tule grass skirts, pine needle headdresses, and feathers of eagles and roadrunners. Their dances mimicked swimming fish and flying birds. They danced to celebrate beauty and the Earth. In caves, they painted pictures of the turtle and the condor. All of nature was honored.

Some villages were ruled by women princesses called wots (wats). One very old story tells of a wot whose people lived on an island. The people wanted to cross over to the mainland, but they didn't know how. The wot made a rainbow bridge for them and told them not to look down as they walked on it or they

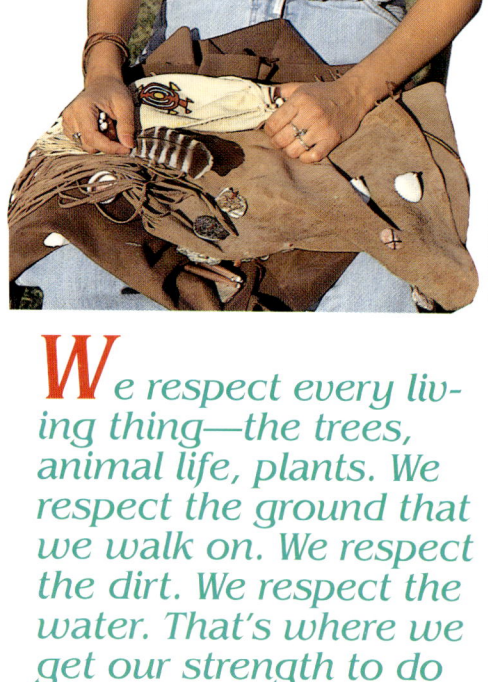

We respect every living thing—the trees, animal life, plants. We respect the ground that we walk on. We respect the dirt. We respect the water. That's where we get our strength to do things. Without this we would not be alive.

—Jacy Romero

The Chumash reservation

would fall into the water and drown. Despite the warning, some looked and fell. Mercifully, she didn't let them drown. Instead, she turned them into dolphins. This is why, to this day, the Chumash people call the dolphins brothers.

Before the Spanish armies came there were thousands of Chumash. In the beginning of the Spanish occupation some members of the tribe cooperated with the newcomers in building Catholic missions along the coast. Those who didn't cooperate were forced to work or were killed. The missionaries didn't understand the Chumash way of life and thought the tribe was uncivilized. The naturalness and beauty of women wearing nothing but grass skirts was seen as sinful. Many of the tribe moved inland to avoid the new ways. Others chose to hide their tribal roots and adopt European ways. There were no great battles, no great wars. The tribe simply began to disappear.

Today, there are only 300 Chumash people on a ninety-nine acre reservation in the mountains near Santa Ynez, California, a two-day walk from the ocean. Others live away from the reservation. This tiny piece of land was "given" to them by the Spanish missionaries. As late as the 1960s there were only a few families on the reservation, and the old ways were close to being lost. Some books even said the tribe was extinct. They were wrong. This tribe and its traditional ways are growing stronger each year. Their native language is again being used by the Chumash and taught to their children. The dances continue. Through the dedication and work of a few families, the Chumash way of life is being renewed.

The Chumash are an inspiration to all people struggling to survive. Like the other tribes in this book, the Chumash hold the Earth and nature at the center of their lives. The survival of the Chumash people and ways holds out hope that each one of us, no matter where our people come from, might be able to rekindle our ancient tribal fires and reclaim our connection to the Earth.

Jacy's daughter, Casandra, in her backyard

Cliffs on the Pacific Ocean near Santa Barbara, California, traditional Chumash territory

JACY ROMERO

Jacy Romero was born in 1965 in Santa Barbara, California. Her father is from the Chumash tribe, her mother is from the Apache and Navajo tribes and is part German. As a child Jacy did not realize she was Native American. Because she looked similar to the Mexican-American children in the town where she grew up, she assumed she was Mexican-American.

When she was nine her father began to teach the children how to dance. He didn't know the Chumash dances, so they danced the dance of the plains Indian.

My Dad knew he was Indian from a young age, but didn't know what kind. He wasn't told until he was about thirty that he belonged to the Chumash tribe. Before that he didn't know exactly how they dressed. He thought all Indians were dressed in buckskin, beads, and breastplates, and wore lots of turquoise.

When Jacy was ten years old the family moved to the Chumash reservation where they have lived ever since. There, the family learned the dances and songs and ceremonial dress of their people.

When I was about thirteen my Dad finally got us into grass skirts. There were six of us girls here at the time.

Until she returned to the reservation, Jacy lived a typical American life. Oddly, it wasn't until she moved back to the reservation that she began to experience discrimination as a Native American. She had come from a town where there was a cultural mix that included Hispanic- and African-Americans. But in the town of Santa Ynez, outside the reservation, most people were Anglo-Americans.

The reservation here had a bad reputation. We were outcasts, and the kids at school teased us. They called me "Indian" and "squaw" and things like that. I'd come home, and my dad would be furious. He'd say:

Jacy prepares to dance

"Be strong. Be proud of who you are." But I had to go to school and spend eight hours with these children. Not all of them were bad, but the loudest ones were. It was awful going to school here when I was growing up. Even the teachers tended to be a little prejudiced.

A change began to happen in the years that followed, and Jacy's younger sisters didn't experience the same problems.

It was starting to be O.K. because there were more and more Indians moving to the reservation. At one time there were about five families on the reservation. As the population grew, they had no choice but to accept us. My children are now going to the same school I did, and there are no problems.

Today, Jacy lives on the reservation with her husband Michael and her three children, Cassie, Angelique, and Michael. One of her sisters lives next door, and one lives across the street. Her father, Tony, lives down the hill behind her.

Jacy in her backyard on the Chumash Reservation

The Chumash have watched the sun set over the Pacific Ocean for thousands of years

JACY'S ART: DANCING IN THE GOOD WAY

When she was eleven, Jacy and her family began to dance together at pow wows, which are gatherings of different tribes. The family eventually took the name Dolphin Dancers.

The dolphins make clicking sounds. We have an instrument that mimics this sound. It is a clap stick. In Chumash it's called a wonsak (WAN•sock). It's made of willow. There's a split right through the middle of the stick. The handle is about the size of your palm. You can slap it on your hand to make the sound of the dolphin. In the dolphin dance, the dancer carries two that he slaps against the calf of his leg. He bends over and pounds the ground with his feet. It's a very fast-moving dance. The dance is done by men, but if a woman wanted to pick up the wonsak and do the dolphin dance, she could.

Many Chumash dances imitate sea creatures, including the swordfish and the barracuda as well as the dolphin. Another dance that Jacy does is the anakchan (a•NOHK•chon) which is a prayer dance for beauty.

Four girls get in a circle. They represent the north, south, east, and west—the four directions. They pray that they grow up to be beautiful and that one day they will find a husband and carry on the tradition.

Jacy's three children are all learning to dance and learning the Chumash language.

My son, who is six, will not put on a grass skirt. I understand. I suppose if I keep bringing him to dances he will eventually say, "Hey, it's O.K." But my daughters love it, and that's a great feeling for me.

The children are learning the meaning of the dances and songs.

We respect every living thing. The trees, animal life, and plants—we get a lot from Mother Earth. We respect the ground that we walk on. We respect

Jacy works on her traditional outfit

the dirt. We respect the water. That's where we get our strength to do things. Without this we would not be alive. We must respect the things that we have here on this Earth. Everything on this Earth has a meaning. We shouldn't destroy any of it. Because God, who we call Shupo, has put all of this on the Earth. That's the way we live. We honor all these things with dances that inspire us and other people to respect and appreciate them.

When Jacy and her family show their dances in public it is not just a performance. They carry with them the spirit of their ancestors who preceded them in the dance.

It is the way of my people to sing and to dance. My people have lived and died so that I can continue to dance. I show our way of life so that it is not forgotten. It is good that I can sing these songs and wear the traditional ceremonial dress out of respect for them.

Jacy dancing at the Pacific Ocean

FIND YOUR TRADITIONS

The Chumash reservation is a place alive with possibility. The children play happily in the streets, and there is a sense of renewal in the air. People like Jacy's father, Tony Romero, have dedicated themselves to rediscovering the wealth of traditions that is the Chumash legacy.

Like her tribe, Jacy has come a long way. When she was a child she knew nothing of her roots. Now she is able to share the Chumash dances and songs with many people. One of her dreams is to dance with her family in Europe.

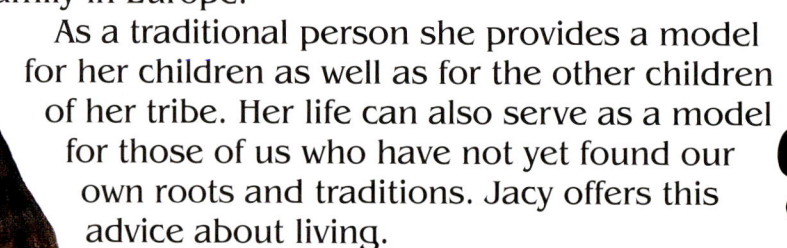

As a traditional person she provides a model for her children as well as for the other children of her tribe. Her life can also serve as a model for those of us who have not yet found our own roots and traditions. Jacy offers this advice about living.

I think that children should always respect their elders and treat them well. Always respect the ground you walk on. If you see someone doing something bad to the Earth or to the animals, don't be afraid to correct them. When you're growing up there is a lot of temptation to ignore your heritage. But that's the time to go out and find your traditions.

Jacy and her children, (left to right) Casandra, Michael, and Angelique

Jodie Winsor

ACTIVITY PAGE

VOICE OF THE DOLPHIN

The Chumash wonsak is a clapping stick that imitates the clicking sound that thedolphins make. This is how you can make and use a wonsak.

Ask an adult to help you make your wonsak.

Step 1. Find a thin straight branch from a tree about 18 to 24 inches long and at least half an inch thick. The Chumash make wonsaks from willow trees. If you don't have a willow, another type of tree will do. Be sure to show respect for the tree by thanking it for its branch and by cutting it off carefully so that the tree is not damaged. You will need a green branch, not a dead one, so the wonsak will be moist and flexible.

Step 2. Carefully saw the branch lenghwise, except for about four inches at the end.

Step 3. To make a handle, tightly wrap colored yarn several times around the end of the branch that hasn't been cut until all four inches are covered with yarn. Leave a piece of yarn about three inches long unwrapped at the end. Apply paste or glue to this loose yarn. Then, wrap it around the stick and hold it in place until the glue starts to dry.

Step 4. When the glue is completely dry hold the wonsak by the handle. To make the sound of the dolphin, gently slap the split end of the stick against your palm. Do it fast and you will hear the clicking that is like the language of the dolphins.

Remember, never use the wonsak to hurt yourself or anyone else. The dolphins are very gentle creatures, and we should follow their way when we imitate them.

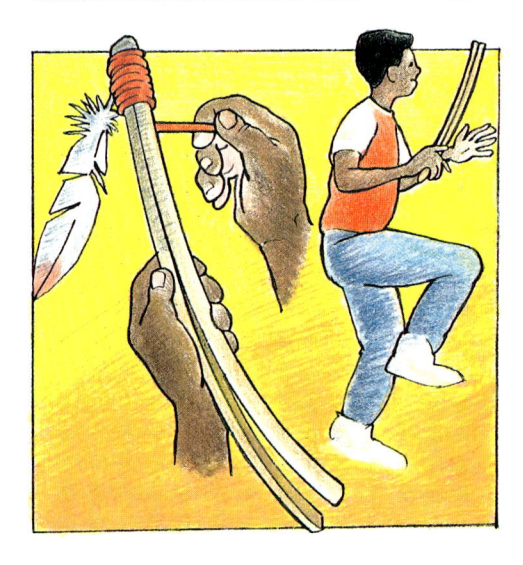

GLOSSARIZED INDEX

Acid rain—rain that is polluted by smoke from factories and power plants, 22

Adobe—a building brick made of mud and straw, 7, 31

Ancestors—your relatives who lived several generations before you were born, 10, 30, 31, 36, 43

Bead work—necklaces, bracelets, dolls, and other art objects made of, or decorated with, beads, 8, 29

Celtic—one of the native tribes that lived in Europe, 5

Ceremony—an act used to mark or celebrate an event or to show respect and gratitude. Native Americans often hold ceremonies that include dancing and singing, 5, 7, 9, 10, 30

Cradleboards, 24, 26, 27

Creation myth—a story, passed down from generation to generation, about how the world began, 6

Culture—the traditions, art, social structure, values, and beliefs of a group of people

Dolphins, 38, 39, 42, 45

Endangered Species—animals and plants that are in danger of being destroyed forever, 17, 22

Etching—an image carved in wood, rock, or other material, 9

Idol—an object that is worshipped, 7

Institute of American Indian Arts—a two-year college in Santa Fe, New Mexico, that is dedicated to teaching Native American arts and crafts, 16, 25

Iroquois Confederacy—a group of five Native American tribes in the northeast, 22

Legend—a story about the distant past that is passed from generation to generation. Legends are usually based on the truth, but, in them, truth is often mixed with fiction, 14

Long houses, 22

Mesa—a large, flat-topped area of land that stands higher than the other land around it. Native tribes often built their settlements on the top of mesas so they could easily see the arrival of herds of animals and groups of other people into their territory, 30

Migration—a mass movement of animals from one region or climate to another, 14

Missionary—a person devoted to converting others to his or her religion or set of beliefs, 7

Mythology—stories, which may or may not be historically true, that explain the social values and attitudes of a group of people, 15

Native Americans—the original inhabitants of North America

Natives—people who were the original human inhabitants of a land, 5

Pow wow—a gathering of Native American tribes, 16, 31, 32, 42

Rainbow Warriors—people of all different colors and races who share a love for the Earth, a desire for a better world, and a willingness to work for both, 4

Reservation—an area of land set aside by the United States government as a homeland for a Native American tribe, 15, 16, 39, 40, 41

Sacred—highly valued, very important, 7, 15

Salmon People—a name given to a group of Native American tribes living in the northwest, 14

Self-esteem—feeling good about oneself, 17, 26

Shaman—a name for a priest or religious leader in native cultures, 8, 10

Spawn—to produce and deposit eggs. Most species of salmon live in the ocean. When it is time for the females to lay their eggs they swim up into rivers that flow into the ocean, 14

Surplus foods—food of a slightly lower quality that is given or sold at a low cost to special groups like schools and poor communities, 33

Traditions—information, beliefs, and customs passed from one generation to another

Tribe—a group of people with a common identity made up of numerous families and different generations

Visions—images of people, things, and other beings that are seen and heard in a person's mind but that are not present in a physical sense, 10

Yarn painting—the art of making images with colored yarn, 8-13

A portion of the proceeds from the sale of this book go to the Rainbow Warrior Fund (administered by the Tides Foundation) for the preservation of native cultures and the environment. These are some of the organizations we support:

    The Huichol Cultural Center, Santiago, Mexico
    Lighthawk: The Environmental Air Force, Santa Fe, New Mexico
    Native Lifeways: Oneida Nation, Amherst, New York

COMMUNICATE

Let us know what you think. Write to the artists. Send poetry, pictures, stories, whatever. Send your name and address. We will put you on our mailing list. Write, right now!

Rainbow Warrior
P.O. Box 9858
Santa Fe, New Mexico 87504

JMP IS PROUD TO ANNOUNCE 4 NEW SERIES FOR YOUNG READERS AGES 8 AND UP

Watch for the arrival of these new series at your local bookstore. Or order direct by calling **1-800-888-7504** and receive our **free** young readers catalog.

BIZARRE & BEAUTIFUL SERIES

A spirited and fun investigation of the mysteries of the five senses in the animal kingdom.

Each title is 8½" x 11", 48 pages, $14.95 hardcover, with color photographs and illustrations throughout.

Bizarre & Beautiful Ears (available 9/93)
Bizarre & Beautiful Eyes (available 9/93)
Bizarre & Beautiful Feelers (available 10/93)
Bizarre & Beautiful Noses (available 9/93)
Bizarre & Beautiful Tongues (available 11/93)

ROUGH AND READY SERIES

Learn about the men and women who settled the American frontier. Explore the myths and legends about these courageous individuals and learn about the environmental, cultural, and economic legacies they left to us.

Each title is written by A. S. Gintzler and is 48 pages, 8½" x 11", $12.95 hardcover, with two-color illustrations and duotone archival photographs.

Rough and Ready Cowboys (available 4/94)
Rough and Ready Homesteaders (available 4/94)
Rough and Ready Prospectors (available 4/94)

RAINBOW WARRIOR ARTISTS SERIES

What is a Rainbow Warrior Artist? It is a person who strives to live in harmony with the Earth and all living creatures, and who tries to better the world while living his or her life in a creative way.

Each title is written by Reavis Moore with a foreword by LeVar Burton, and is 8½" x 11", 48 pages, $14.95 hardcover, with color photographs and illustrations.

Native Artists of Africa (available 1/94)
Native Artists of North America

AMERICAN ORIGINS SERIES

Many of us are the third and fourth generation of our families to live in America. Learn what our great-great grandparents experienced when they arrived here and how much of our lives are still intertwined with theirs.

Each title is 48 pages, 8½" x 11", $12.95 hardcover, with two-color illustrations and duotone archival photographs.

Tracing Our German Roots, Leda Silver (available 12/93)
Tracing Our Irish Roots, Sharon Moscinski (available 10/93)
Tracing Our Italian Roots, Kathleen Lee (available 10/93)
Tracing Our Jewish Roots, Miriam Sagan (available 12/93)

ORDERING INFORMATION
Please check your local bookstore for our books, or call 1-800-888-7504 to order direct from us. All orders are shipped via UPS; see chart to calculate your shipping charge for U.S. destinations. **No P.O. Boxes please; we must have a street address to ensure delivery.** If the book you request is not available, we will hold your check until we can ship it. Foreign orders will be shipped surface rate unless otherwise requested; please enclose $3.00 for the first item and $1.00 for each additional item.

METHODS OF PAYMENT
Check, money order, American Express, MasterCard, or Visa. We cannot be responsible for cash sent through the mail. For credit card orders, include your card number, expiration date, and your signature, or call (800) 888-7504. American Express card orders can be shipped only to billing address of cardholder. Sorry, no C.O.D.'s. Residents of sunny New Mexico, add 6.125% tax to total.

Address all orders and inquiries to:
John Muir Publications
P.O. Box 613
Santa Fe, NM 87504
(505) 982-4078
(800) 888-7504

For U.S. Orders Totaling	Add
Up to $15.00	$4.25
$15.01 to $45.00	$5.25
$45.01 to $75.00	$6.25
$75.01 or more	$7.25

MORE OF YOUR FAVORITE JOHN MUIR PUBLICATIONS BOOKS
FOR A FREE CATALOG CALL 1-800-888-7504

EXTREMELY WEIRD SERIES

All of the titles are written by Sarah Lovett, 8 1/2" x 11", 48 pages, $9.95 paperbacks, with color photographs and illustrations.

Extremely Weird Bats
Extremely Weird Birds
Extremely Weird Endangered Species
Extremely Weird Fishes
Extremely Weird Frogs
Extremely Weird Insects
Extremely Weird Mammals (available 8/93)
Extremely Weird Micro Monsters (available 8/93)
Extremely Weird Primates
Extremely Weird Reptiles
Extremely Weird Sea Creatures
Extremely Weird Snakes (available 8/93)
Extremely Weird Spiders

X-RAY VISION SERIES

Each title in the series is 8 1/2" x 11", 48 pages, $9.95 paperback, with color photographs and illustrations and written by Ron Schultz.

Looking Inside the Brain
Looking Inside Cartoon Animation
Looking Inside Caves and Caverns
 (available 11/93)
Looking Inside Sports Aerodynamics
Looking Inside Sunken Treasure
Looking Inside Telescopes and the Night Sky

THE KIDDING AROUND TRAVEL GUIDES

All of the titles listed below are 64 pages and $9.95 paperbacks, except for *Kidding Around the National Parks* and *Kidding Around Spain*, which are 108 pages and $12.95 paperbacks.

Kidding Around Atlanta
Kidding Around Boston, 2nd ed.
Kidding Around Chicago, 2nd ed.
Kidding Around the Hawaiian Islands
Kidding Around London
Kidding Around Los Angeles
Kidding Around the National Parks
 of the Southwest
Kidding Around New York City, 2nd ed.
Kidding Around Paris
Kidding Around Philadelphia
Kidding Around San Diego
Kidding Around San Francisco
Kidding Around Santa Fe
Kidding Around Seattle
Kidding Around Spain
Kidding Around Washington, D.C., 2nd ed.

MASTERS OF MOTION SERIES

Each title in the series is 10 1/4" x 9", 48 pages, $9.95 paperback, with color photographs and illustrations.

How to Drive an Indy Race Car
David Rubel
How to Fly a 747
Tim Paulson
How to Fly the Space Shuttle
Russell Shorto

THE KIDS EXPLORE AMERICA SERIES

Each title is written by kids for kids by the Westridge Young Writers Workshop, 7" x 9", with photographs and illustrations by the kids.

Kids Explore America's Hispanic Heritage
112 pages, $7.95 paper
Kids Explore America's African-American Heritage
128 pages, $8.95 paper
Kids Explore the Gifts of Children with Special Needs
112 pages, $8.95 paper (available 2/94)
Kids Explore America's Japanese Heritage
112 pages, $8.95 paper (available 4/94)

ENVIRONMENTAL TITLES

Habitats: Where the Wild Things Live
Randi Hacker and Jackie Kaufman
8 1/2" x 11", 48 pages, color illustrations, $9.95 paper

The Indian Way: Learning to Communicate with Mother Earth
Gary McLain
7" x 9", 114 pages, illustrations, $9.95 paper

Rads, Ergs, and Cheeseburgers: The Kids' Guide to Energy and the Environment
Bill Yanda
7" x 9", 108 pages, two-color illustrations, $13.95 paper

The Kids' Environment Book: What's Awry and Why
Anne Pedersen
7" x 9", 192 pages, two-color illustrations, $13.95 paper